CW01192069

TALES OF MOOR AND STREAM

Colonel's Pool, River Kjarra, Iceland

Charles van Straubenzee

COUNTRYSIDE BOOKS
NEWBURY BERKSHIRE

First published 2021
© Charles van Straubenzee 2021

All rights reserved. No part of this publication may be reproduced, stored in a retrieval system, or transmitted by any means, electronic, mechanical, photocopying, recording or otherwise, without the prior written permission of the copyright holder and publishers.

Photographs by the author

Front cover – One each for Charles and Penny van Straubenzee fishing the Washerwoman and Macallan, River Carron, Braelangwell.

Back cover – Charlie's Pool, River Carron, Braelangwell.

ISBN 978 1 84674 406 8

Published by Countryside Books
Produced by The Letterworks Ltd., Reading
Typeset by KT Designs, St Helens
Printed by Holywell Press, Oxford

CONTENTS

PREFACE	4
INTRODUCTION	5
CLUNES	8
● STORIES FROM THE HILL AT CLUNES	9
BRAELANGWELL	13
SALMON FISHING	19
A STRANGE KIND OF MADNESS	21
SALMON FISHING IN SCOTLAND	23
● THE WEST COAST	23
● THE NORTH COAST	26
● THE EAST COAST	29
SALMON FISHING IN ICELAND	38
GROUSE SHOOTING – ENGLAND	47
GROUSE SHOOTING – SCOTLAND	50
STALKING	54
DOGS	59
THE BEST DAY'S SPORT OF MY LIFE	64
A LIST OF OUTSTANDING DAYS	66
GROUSE MOORS ON WHICH I HAVE SHOT	69
SCOTTISH SALMON RIVERS THAT I HAVE FISHED	70
ICELANDIC SALMON RIVERS THAT I HAVE FISHED	71
ESTATES THAT I HAVE STALKED ON IN SCOTLAND	71
EXTRACTS FROM BOOKS WHICH I HAVE MUCH ENJOYED	72
● THE HIGH TOPS	72
● A LADY DEERSTALKER	74

PREFACE

The idea of putting this book together was largely the inspiration of my nephew Thomas. He has been extremely keen on field sports from the early years of his life, and has participated in much grander shoots than I.

However, he would still drive many a mile and appreciate a day's hedgerowing at the back-end of the season. He also much enjoys casting a fly in the search of a salmon, and I was keen to be present when he caught his first fish. That never happened, but I did get close to achieving my goal. We were on the Tweed at Middle Mertoun and I put him into a pool in front of myself, and tied on a Comet fly. After he had gone down some 50 yards I followed him into the pool with exactly the same fly on the line. After a short time I hooked and landed a fish which is the only one that I wished I had not caught.

Thomas van Straubenzee

We have spent many an hour reminiscing, and one day he suggested that I put down on paper some of the stories of my experiences, places that I have been to, and people that I have met on the way. I have enjoyed an amazing sporting life.

There is a story behind the choice of the title to this book. A good friend of mine, Anthony Clegg and I spent many a day on the banks of rivers in Scotland, especially the Naver. When in London, where we both worked and resided, we we would often have lunch or dinner and basically recount 'Tales of Moor and Stream'. Sadly he recently died but this photograph shows him holding a 22lb salmon caught in the Back Braes of Upper Mertoun.

Anthony Clegg

INTRODUCTION

A change of venue for family summer holidays was decided upon in the early 1960s. We had been to Bembridge, Isle of Wight, for a long time and we had grown out of sandcastles, and were not that keen on sailing.

The Highlands in Scotland beckoned and in 1963 my father, with others, took Conaglen, an estate roughly the other side of Loch Linnhe from Fort William. The sport consisted of fishing the river Cona, and walking up grouse and ptarmigan. That was the theory but we shot three brace of ptarmigan and caught a few salmon on the last day. We had tried with flies, spinners and every other lure, but to no avail. The retired keeper said that each family could take one fish home, and then showed us how it was done. All that I would say is that it was most exciting!

The following year we went to Balnacoil on the north side of the Brora and Blackwater. The estate was the most westerly of three owned by the Tyser family. The other two were Gordonbush and Kintradwell. Balnacoil had everything that a keen sportsman required. If it rained, we fished, and if the river was not in order, then we walked up grouse. Stalking was also available and we were allowed five stags.

Balnacoil Lodge

Grouse shooting at Balnacoil

The fishing consisted of the lower Brora on Tuesdays and Fridays, and above the loch up to where the river divided on the other days. We also had the Blackwater up to Ben Armine.

On one particular day when there had been a lot of rain, I was fishing with my brother, Alexander, on the Long Pool. We could hear a sort of rumble up the strath, which, unbeknown to us, was the large amount of rainwater having come down the burns and joined the river, and for a time, I hooked a fish with every cast until eventually one stayed on, which I landed. The ghillie then took Alexander and put him on a rock in the pool from where he could cast. A short while later a wall of water came round the corner and would have taken my brother away downstream. The ghillie ran and grabbed him before disaster struck.

I believe that I learnt a great deal of fieldcraft during the three weeks we spent there. I caught my first salmon on a fly, I shot my first stag and I was introduced to shooting over dogs. We had the use of two English setters, Royal, old and wise, and Mark, young and very keen!

The shooting was all walked up, with or without dogs. We shot something over 100 brace during our holiday. The fishing produced about 50 salmon and we shot three stags.

My first stalking experience was at the top of the Achaness Burn, not far from one of the Helmsdale estates. I was armed with a .303 rifle, open sights, and the 'furniture' cut down. The stalker, Alistair Mackintosh, selected a stag, I fired and he remarked that my shot was true. The beast just stood still and he said that I should give it another round. Where I aimed, I cannot remember, but the bullet entered its head just behind its ear.

The second day's stalking was beyond the bothy, and we unsuccessfully tried to get into a group of stags, of which one was a Royal. They eventually moved into a much bigger lot of beasts that were heading away from us across a bit of land that would give us no cover. Alistair, who was also carrying a rifle, said that if he put a shot over their heads, the echo might send them back towards us. He fired a shot, and that is exactly what happened. A long string of beasts trotted past us without stopping, and so Alistair shot a stag at the front of the column, hoping to slow them down. I had no idea what to do, so I was told to have a go at one at the back, which I did, and a stag fell.

Incidentally, I had been told that I should not shoot the Royal as it was a sackable offence to take such a beast off the hill. However, I had unfortunately felled the said stag. Sadly one of the antlers was shot off the head, and buried, and the head was cut off and put in a fox trap. If anyone looks in the Game Book at Balnacoil, the entry says

My first stag shot at Balnacoil

'Single horned beast with six points'. That was the only Royal that I have ever shot.

One of the most interesting people that I ever met in Scotland, and who lived in Brora was Megan Boyd. She was an internationally famous salmon fly tyer, and she tied hundreds of flies for me. The collection, now in the Flyfishers' Club, came from myself. She kindly made flies for me for many years.

The two estates that I went to more than any others were Clunes and Braelangwell. The former I was invited to for some 50 years, and the latter we took for just under 30 years. They both had a massive influence on my sporting life.

CLUNES

Clunes Lodge

I first went to Clunes, one of the Atholl estates in September 1966. It had been taken by my friend, David Barnett's father for a few years prior to this. We were there for a couple of days and both got a stag.

The following year I was up in August to walk up grouse. I remember arriving at Blair Atholl station, off the night sleeper, very early in the morning. I did not know that the lodge did not have mains electricity, so when I turned on the light in my appointed bedroom, the generator started up, making a real racket. Off went the light.

I was somewhat apprehensive at breakfast as I knew not many of the other guests. Everything was very formal and regimented. Breakfast was at 8 o'clock, not 7.59 nor 8.01, and dinner was the same. Wheels rolled for the hill at nine, and all those going were booted and spurred a good 15 minutes earlier. We would return in time for a substantial tea and then don our tennis gear for a set or two down at Blair Castle. Afterwards there would be a race to bathe and put on a black tie and have time to down a glass of whisky. There would always be a table or two of bridge to finish the day.

In the 1960s and 1970s the grouse shooting tended to go up and down in five year cycles. When there were enough birds we would have a few driven days, but

On the hill at Clunes

most were walked up. There would usually be eight guns in the line, along with some of the ladies in the lodge, and a couple of people to pick up, and of course the keeper.

Eventually the grouse population declined and I believe there were two main reasons. The low ground became a wintering home for some 1,000 stags, which ruined the ground. Secondly, it was decided to put in miles of hill drains which mostly were about 50 yards apart. If a hen grouse had her nest in the middle, she has only 25 yards to go before she and her brood had to cross one of them. If it is wet, the chicks fall into the water, and that is the end of a nice covey.

During the 50 plus years that I was kindly invited to stay at Clunes, there were only three stalkers. Sandy Reid, who went to the castle at Blair, followed by his brother Colin, who sadly died in his early 50s, and then Ronnie Hepburn.

Tuesdays and Fridays were not shooting days. There was fishing on either the Garry or the Tilt, and a stalking party made for the hill. A certain amount of golf was played at Blair Atholl, which had a 9-hole course.

STORIES FROM THE HILL AT CLUNES

When we stayed at Braelangwell, I used to take a day on the hill at Clunes. It would take me about two hours to drive to Colin Reid's house where I would have a large breakfast, and then off to the hill. In 1992, we stalked a large herd of stags behind the bothy, who were all lying down. Eventually they got up, and a stag was chosen, but I could only see the top half of its body. I took the shot, and did something that

Johnny Greenall, C.F.vS, Colin Campbell Golding, David Harvey

I am not particularly proud of, but it happened. I missed the intended beast, and killed a stag and a hind behind. Later in the day, I got another one.

The following year, I went down again and had one shot, and got two stags. So, in two days, I had three shots and got four stags and one hind.

In July 1982, I was invited to fish on the Dionard by Anthony Duckworth-Chad. As it was such a long way north I asked Colin Reid if I could have a bed in Clunes Lodge, so I would break up the journey. He told me to come early on the Saturday morning and he would arrange a day's fishing on the Tay. At the end of an unsuccessful day I returned to his house, where I had a large meal with him, Liz and his three children.

When we had finished, he asked me if I would like to go stalking, as the restaurant at the Castle needed a beast. Away we went up the Bruar road and I shot a stag at about 10pm in broad daylight. We returned home and he and I drank a bottle of whisky and, at some time, I said that I had to get my head down.

I knew that upstairs were two bedrooms, one for the children, and one for Colin and Liz. I said that I would sleep on the sofa or in a room at the lodge. Colin said, in a quite authoritative way, that was not going to happen – I was put in the double bed, and the Reids were in the other room. I was somewhat embarrassed, but you cannot buy a relationship like that.

Frequently I would leave Clunes and drive south to Wensleydale in Yorkshire to shoot grouse at Bolton Castle. On one occasion, I was told that we would be shooting with two guns as there were plenty of birds. I did not have a pair of guns,

CLUNES

Ronnie Hepburn outside the larder at Clunes

but my brother was staying further up the A9 and I knew that he was taking the night sleeper south on the following Saturday. Unfortunately the train no longer stopped at Blair Atholl, but I knew Jimmy, who was in charge of everything at the station. I drove down to see him, and asked if there was any chance that he could stop the train as I had something to collect from it. He told me that this was feasible and I pressed a small brown envelope into his hand. I then rang my brother to warn him of my cunning plan, and made sure that he was agreeable to lending me his gun.

In the evening, having changed for dinner, I drove down to the station, which was in total darkness, to find Jimmy in his room with a brazier, belting out enormous amounts of heat. Some five or ten minutes before the expected arrival of the train, I got out onto the platform to see far in the distance this well-lit snake coming down the tracks. All of a sudden all the lights go on, the signal goes to red, and here am I, in a dinner jacket, Labrador sitting next to me, standing to attention. The train stops, down goes a window, and a gun gets passed through. The signal goes green, and away chugs the train. That would not happen nowadays.

One or two vignettes spring to mind of occurrences while staying at Clunes. In the early 1970s there were quite a few blackcock on the hill, and it was decided to have a drive in the woods, just above the A9. The sun was out and it was a beautiful vista of heather and silver birch trees. During the drive a covey of blackcock flew over the guns and a few were shot. What remains in my memory was the sun on the feathers of the birds, and all the other wonderful colours. Very Thorburnesque!

One other memory was a day's driven grouse on the low ground. We did four drives in the morning and two in the afternoon. I think the bag was somewhere in the region of 45 brace, and so I should have had some shooting during the day. In fact I fired one shot in the last drive, and missed!

A very sad and memorable event happened on August 19, 1980. We were out on the high ground on the east side of the Meall Dubh, walking up grouse. We moved on to the Sron na Faiceachan where we had our piece. Afterwards we climbed sharply uphill before lining out. The first bird to get up was in front of Cedric Barnett, who shot it, and almost immediately after we moved forwards again, he fell dead having had a heart attack. I could take anyone to the spot where he died, as it was in a green runner that is visible from miles away. Most of the people in the line ran off the hill to seek assistance, but I remained with David and Pussy Barnett. Unfortunately the mist came down, and so there was no chance of getting a helicopter in to help. The law was in those days that a body could not be moved until a doctor and the police had arrived on scene. The three of us stayed on the hill for some hours occasionally firing shots to guide people to where we sat. Eventually Cedric Barnett left the high ground strapped to a deer saddle on the back of a garron.

BRAELANGWELL

Braelangwell Lodge

We first set foot in Braelangwell Lodge in 1978. Basically the sport consisted of five rods on the left bank of the Carron which was split into two beats, as we shared the stretch with the other bank which was Gruinards. If we were on the bottom beat in the morning, we were up in the afternoon, and vice versa on the following day. There was an odd grouse to walk up, and I usually had a couple of days stalking. We were admirably looked after by Ronnie Ross, a fount of knowledge outside, and by Margaret, his wife, indoors.

The first year was a blank, but in 1979 we caught 42 fish, 21 in each week we were there. We had five spates in the fortnight, so the river was in good order most days. The following year we had 21 in the first week and then nothing thereafter. The river fished well enough, but then we saw some diseased fish which turned the rest off completely. We went to Braelangwell for 29 years, and when Ronnie retired,

Ronnie Ross, Braelangwell Keeper

and our wonderful cook decided not to come again, we thought it was time to move on.

On one occasion when the Carron was in full spate, I thought it would be a good idea to go over the hill to catch up with the ghillies on the Oykel. When I got to the bottom of Beat 4, I could see a couple fishing the Bank Pool, and he was playing a fish. His wife was having some difficulty in netting the salmon, so I stopped the car and offered my services. I happened to be wearing a pair of plus fours made from the same tweed as all the ghillies and stalkers wore. I netted the fish and went back to my car, and I could see that the fishers were bewildered by my appearance. I wore the right clothing for an employee of the estate, but my car and accent did not fit.

When I returned to our lodge, I asked someone where everybody had gone, only to be told they had all rushed to the river and were catching fish. I had been informed that no one caught anything at the height the river was. How wrong they were.

Life in the lodge was always relaxed and fun. My father did not like taking a piece to the river for lunch, and so we all returned for a good gin and tonic and got our feet under the table. Returning to the river at whatever time the height of the water dictated was a movable objective. I remember one of our guests was rather peeved that she and her husband had not fished the 'Washerwoman' much, so I said 'have the pool for the afternoon'. They returned fishless for a late cup of tea, and I said some time later, that I might pop down there for a quick flick of the fly. I came back after about half an hour having got a fish almost immediately. The good lady was not amused.

My brother, Alexander, in 1990 caught a 19lb fish in the same pool, and landed it in some ten minutes. The following day I decided to go down there before breakfast, and hooked a fish at about 7.30am. It was an extremely strong, but dour salmon, and half an hour into the fight I had made little progress. At half past eight I wondered if anybody might miss me at the breakfast table. However, shortly afterwards it came in, and landed. It weighed 18lb.

One of the best days that I had on the Carron was acting as ghillie for my friend Johnny Greenall. On his first day the river was in good order and he caught three

The team on 17 September 2004 (top row) Johnny Greenall, Jeremy Delmar-Morgan, Colin Campbell Golding, Robert Bigland, C.F.vS (bottom row) Mary Delmar-Morgan, Liz Campbell Golding, P.J.vS, Biddy Bigland

fish, which were all hooked in pools where he would never have known how to fish. The first of the day was at the tail of Lower Craigs, the second under the right bank of Morail, and finally at the bottom of the Banks. Everyone was very happy.

Monday September 17, 2004 was the best day that we ever had on the river. There were 11 people in the lodge and on that day nine of them landed a fish. Penny never touched a fish all week, and so I said to her on Saturday, 'Where would you like to go?' With no hesitation she said Gardeners, which I would not have chosen. She caught two salmon in about half an hour.

One of the regular rods was General Sir John Mogg, my father's best friend and my godfather. He was a very senior officer, in all departments, and had a great sense of humour. One day he returned to the lodge and I asked him how he had got on. He had been fishing the Banks, where one normally caught fish halfway down or at the tail. He told me that he had got three fish right at the top in the rough water. I was amazed, and he turned to me and said 'You've got to be good!'

H.H.vS and John Mogg, after lunch!

Morail Falls, Braelangwell

Some years we would take the fishing on other beats, which included Glencalvie, Amat and Gruinards. On one day I was fishing the right-hand bank of the Morail where I hooked a fish halfway down. There was a strong flow of water, so any sized fish would give one a good fight. At some point the fish decided that it was going to leave the pool, and I had no chance of following. I had read somewhere that if you rip the line off the reel, the fish will believe that it has been released and it will stop its run. That is exactly what happened and the fish stopped just short of the tail of the pool. I reeled in the slack line and it was still on, and eventually landed.

Another time I was fishing the Falls pool at Glencalvie. You cast off a high platform at the top of the pool, and often the best place to hook a fish is at the tail. Eventually, my fly came round at the bottom, and I felt a good pull, then nothing. Exactly the same thing happened on the next cast, so I thought that I would change tactics, and if it occurred again I would strike and hope for the best. Everything went to plan except that rather than hooking a salmon, I had hooked a bunch of plastic flowers.

I have only once been praised for catching a fish, and it was when I was in the Gruinards Run, casting from the left-hand bank. I was about a third of the way down when I hooked a salmon and landed it. I released it and stood for a moment until I had the feeling that I was being watched. Across the river, a lady was sitting on a bench, and smiling at my success. She said, 'Thank you for making a bad day somewhat better'. It was Jean Matterson's mother, whose own mother had died very recently. Jean was the owner of Gruinards.

Team photo at Braelangwell. 3 Duckworth-Chads, 2 Harveys and 8 van Straubenzees

In 1980, I was walking down the riverbank having fished Burnmouth, and noticed a fish jump the rough water above Shepherds. I decided to have a few casts and to my slight surprise I hooked and landed a small grilse. It took some years to learn how to fish it correctly, which was to divide the pool into four bits and fish each one separately. The next year the team caught about a third of all the fish from that pool, and I thought it deserved to be a named pool, and now it is on the map as 'Charlie's Pool'.

Charlie's Pool, Braelangwell

I had several days on the hill with Ronnie Ross, and shot a few stags. The average weight of the beasts was over 15 stone, which is quite high for an east coast estate. One incident still amuses me on reflection. We came off the hill well after dark, as the light was very poor when I took the shot. I could only see the stag through the telescope, and not with the naked eye. Anyway, on return, Ronnie was dressing the beast, and I went to get a very large glass of whisky for him and myself. They disappeared quickly and I reloaded. After a late dinner with the odd glass of wine, I settled into some vintage port as my mother went upstairs to bed. The following morning my father took me to one side and said, 'Your mother thinks that you have a drink problem.'

We occasionally walked up the odd grouse but never shot many, perhaps two or three brace.

SALMON FISHING

I think that I am more fascinated by salmon fishing than any other sporting pastime. I feel that there are more experts in this field that I have listened to, or read about their pontifications on this wonderful art of catching this king/queen of fish. The fact is that no one knows why a salmon takes any sort of lure. Salmon flies that I used in the 1960s and 1970s are pretty well never seen in fly boxes now. I remember some years ago showing my flies to a ghillie, whose comment was 'useless'. I have sometimes felt that the local tackle shops were in league with the ghillies.

I was told that an eminent fisher said, 'When I had caught 500 fish I knew everything about salmon fishing, but when I had caught 1,000 I knew nothing!' Great words. Even when conditions look to be ideal at breakfast time, you can be made to look quite stupid. Once when fishing on the Carron, I was asked for my prediction for the day. There had been a good spate overnight and the river had now settled back to a good height. I thought that anything between five or ten fish should be on the cards. We never touched a single fish.

I used to collect books on field sports, and one writer gave his opinions on what went into hooking a salmon. It was 60% luck, 30% knowing the river, and 10% skill. I am sure some will quibble about the percentages, but I feel that is about right.

If someone were to ask me, 'What is the best thing in all field sports?' my answer, without doubt, would be the take of a salmon. I can honestly say that the split second that a fish takes my fly, is still as exciting as it was in 1964. There is so much more to fishing than just catching fish. If you are a countryman or naturalist there is much going on. Birdlife, flowers and usually tranquillity.

When I started fishing for salmon, I was taught to cast downstream at roughly 45 degrees and let the fly come round, draw the line in, take a step and repeat the process. There are various alternatives depending on the speed of the current and the depth of the water. But my eyes were opened to many variations of how and where to put my fly when I went to Iceland. Casting upstream and hand-lining faster than the current can be most productive. I would suggest that anything is worth trying.

The beauty of salmon fishing is there are many unknowns as to the reason why salmon take a fly – and long may that last!

In 1967 I fished the Dinnet beat on the Dee, where I caught my first big fish, an 18lb bar of silver. The main thing that I remember was that we had an extremely dour ghillie whose nickname was 'Creeping Death'. We went en famille to Applecross on the west coast in September where we caught quite a number of fish.

The following year we were at Uppat on the south bank of the Brora, below the loch. Besides having a ghillie, we had the services of Willie Gunn, made famous because of his great salmon fly. We had some days shooting on both Uppat and Dunrobin.

Willie Gunn, A.deL.vS, W.H.vS, A.H.vS and C.F.vS on the Brora

In 1969 and 1970, I was invited to stay by Jessie Tyser at Gordonbush. Each day we walked up grouse, and after tea we went to the river. We had some wonderful days on the hill, and usually shot between 30 and 40 brace. No women were invited – everyone was involved in sport all day. We were all fairly young except for Jim Pilkington, a great sportsman and a great enthusiast.

One day I was fishing the Well Pool on the lower Brora and hooked a fish at the top. It took off downstream where my hostess was casting. She said, 'What are you doing down here? You are spoiling the pool for me. Put your rod over your shoulder and take the fish back to where you hooked it.' It followed me like a dog on a lead.

Below the lodge, and across the road, was a field of barley stooks. I was informed that grouse flighted off the hill in the evening to eat the grain. So I went down and took up my position behind a wall. Unfortunately not a single bird came, but it was an interesting concept. I believe Thorburn painted a picture of blackgame sitting on stooks.

The following few years we went to the Oykel, staying in a variety of different places ranging from a cottage in Ullapool, the Oykel Bridge Hotel and a marvellous small house called Craggie Cottage. The head ghillie then was George Ross who, in my opinion, is the best caster of a salmon fly that I have ever seen.

A STRANGE KIND OF MAGIC

It was during my first trip to Iceland, some years ago, that I was introduced to a great many new and varied ways of tying salmon flies. Colours that seemed outrageous when compared with traditional patterns, not to mention a judicious use of synthetic flash and some innovative sizes, shapes and weights, all had that fish-catching magic. It was that same magic that I hoped to harness when I began devising the Strawberry Mackenzie. The name for the fly comes from the trick I use when explaining how to pronounce my last name: *Straub-enzee* like the first part of strawberry and the second part of Mackenzie.

I was extremely lucky to begin my salmon-fishing career on the Brora in the early 1960s, lucky because Megan Boyd tied all my flies and Willie Gunn sometimes ghillied for us. We fished with Green Highlanders, Blue Charms and Silver Doctors. Every so often a new fly would appear, something that had a very different style to the accepted patterns and which fast became a favourite, such as the General Practitioner or Ally's Shrimp. The Strawberry Mackenzie borrows something from both these patterns, with the dyed-orange golden pheasant tippets behind the hackle-fibre wing. I wanted the fly to incorporate all the bright colours and flashy materials I was unused to and enlisted the help of Iain Wilson at the Borders Gunroom, St Boswells, in the tying. Together we concocted the finished article.

Of course, no amount of design will make up for a fly that doesn't catch. I believed the Strawberry Mackenzie, with its bright colours, would work well in the coloured water of a spate when the orange, magenta and pink would stand out well against the sediment in the water.

On the Halladale in September 2015 I encountered just such conditions. In that first outing I caught six salmon and rose or lost several more. An auspicious start. In July 2016 I had the opportunity to fish one of the middle Tweed beats where we found the water to be coloured, but not dirty. I landed a fresh 14lb fish in the morning followed by another later on. The next day I had two more. On the third day I thought that I would try a different fly, but after a fruitless few hours I returned to the Strawberry Mackenzie and landed another big salmon.

I believe that the combination of colours in the fly, the magenta and orange in the wind and tail, the golden pheasant tippets and the dual-colour body of pink fritz and fine black chenille ribbed with silver wire creates good contrast and is highly visible. The added advantage of using pink and magenta in the dressing is that it may stimulate a response from fish that have already seen a large number of Cascades, Willie Gunns and other patterns with a predominance of black, orange and yellow. I would use this fly on double or treble hooks in sizes 6 to 10 or as a conehead tube. In coloured water, anywhere from a falling spate to a steady flow it has proved extremely effective for me and I encourage you to give it a try, too.

Article published in *Trout & Salmon* magazine in February 2017.

SALMON FISHING IN SCOTLAND

THE WEST COAST

Since 1963, I have been lucky enough to fish on 41 rivers in Scotland. Some I have been to for a single day and some I have been to for decades. I might also have only cast into a few pools on one particular river, but on the Tweed I have fished 14 different beats.

Anyway, I thought that I would start with the bottom river on the west coast and move northwards, then eastwards and then down the coast to the Tweed. The first on the list is the Stinchar where Penny and I stayed with Richard and Jo Wellesley at Knockdolian on a couple of occasions. The first time we went the river was in good condition, but by mid-morning I had not touched anything. A man appeared who clearly knew the river well, and said that I needed to cast much more down the stream, rather than at 45°. I caught three fish in quick succession in a pool called Lynn Paeth.

The second visit was very low water, but the previous day someone had been to Blackstone and been successful. Having been advised what to do, Penny and I set off to the pool. There is a very large rock on the right bank, on which Penny lay, looking into the water. Just downstream, she could clearly see about 25 salmon lying in water that was almost static. I went to the other bank, and put on an intermediate line and a tiny fly. I then cast out so that the line and fly would sink down to just in front of the fish. I then would hand-line as fast as possible, and occasionally a salmon would peel off and follow the fly. It was extremely exciting as I got a running commentary from Penny and sometimes the fish would follow to within a few feet of where I stood. I landed three fish eventually and I have not had an experience like that again.

Following on northwards we went with the Campbell Goldings to Arran where we had fishings on the Iorsa and the Machrie. I remember little about either river except they were both unproductive. Then came the rivers Awe and Etive, neither of which gave up a fish of any sort. The Awe would be a serious river, in my opinion. In the past it yielded a number of big salmon. The Etive was much smaller and I would think would be great fun after a spate.

After the Cona, about which I have written, elsewhere, we come to the Lochy. This river used to be the pride of the west coast of Scotland, but from the early 1960s catches dropped by about 73%. It could be quite an intimidating river to fish, and on one occasion Penny was casting from a steep shingle bank in the water, and every step took her further into the deepening pool. It made her more than anxious, and finally reduced her to tears. Luckily her brave husband was on hand to help her clamber out. Only one fish was caught by the whole party, but a lasting memory was the sight of Ben Nevis whilst on Beat 4.

The Arnisdale flows into Loch Hourn just south of the lodge, which is a field away from the sea. The river is quite small by any standards, and therefore needs rain. We had one spate during our stay, and I had a very special time starting somewhere near the top of the river, and slowly fishing downstream. We had a leisurely lunch in a bothy, seated in old armchairs. At the end of the day I had caught three salmon, two sea trout and a good sized brown trout. One of the fish that I landed was the first fish from a pool named Clachach, which had recently been built.

Two other memories were from sea trips that we took most days to check lobster and crab pots. These were re-baited with mackerel that we caught in very large amounts, because there was a salmon farm in front of the lodge, with some 20 pens holding nearly a million salmon. The mackerel would feed on the excess food for the fish, and on one day we caught about 250 mackerel. The other memory was spying in a field not far from the sea, a group of some 16 stags whose heads were the best of such a large group that I have ever seen. I would think that the vast majority were Royals or better.

The Applecross is another of those small spate rivers that, when in good order,

C.F.vS playing a fish in Clachach on the River Arnisdale

are able to produce great sport. In 1967 we went en famille to stay with John and Jean Wills, and had several days of rain. I think we caught a good number of fish, and my father had one bumper morning when everyone else was on the hill. The previous day my brother Alexander went stalking and as he took his shot the stag took a step forward, and so was hit too far back. The beast disappeared and it was decided that every able person in the lodge would walk in line to try and find the beast the following day. We were unsuccessful and returned for lunch to find that my father, who was the only rod on the river, had caught seven salmon.

The Kinlochewe I fished for a day if that, whilst staying in a lodge which had mostly stalking and a boat on Loch Maree.

Dickie Skilbeck with his first salmon

In 1995 Penny kindly took a lodge called Eilean Darach on the Dundonnell river, and also the fishings on the Gruinard. I think the Dundonnell is the fastest rising and falling river that I have come across. One day I thought, after a good fall of rain, that I would fish the Gruinard in the morning and come back to the Dundonnell after lunch. Alas the spate was over when I returned.

We had a great time on the Gruinard and caught quite a few fish. Dickie Skilbeck got his first salmon, and I had a most interesting encounter with a fish in the Middle Rockies. The ghillie was on the bank, high above the river, and could see everything in the pool below as the water was quite clear. He could see me, the fly at the end of my leader and the salmon. When my fly got to the fish, he saw it open its mouth and take the shrimp fly. 'He's taken it' came the shout from above, and I felt nothing. This happened three times, before the fish attached itself properly. If I had not had my spotter, I would never have caught it.

We fished the Broom as guests of the Troughtons, I think. Then on up to the Ullapool, which came with the lease of Rhidorroch. I never caught a fish on the river, but I did try to catch one on a worm. It is something that I have never done, which is a sadness, as I believe it to be an art. One thing I do remember is having a stalk on my own without a rifle. Outside the lodge was a loch, and on the far side was a steep terraced wood. I could see that there were deer feeding in amongst the trees,

P.J.vS

so I thought it would be fun to see if I could get close to them. Eventually I found a ledge that I could lie on, and waited for the deer to come along below me. This they did, and I wasn't prepared for them to be so close which was some 10 to 15 yards underneath my position. They never knew that I was there, and fed on undisturbed. It was magical to be able to witness these animals with not a care in the world.

The Grimersta is a river system that I never really got acquainted with. I went firstly with Colin Campbell Golding and foul-hooked a 10lb fish in the first loch and that was exciting. All the other fish that I caught in various visits were from the river. I was never successful in the locks, and all that I would say is that I would prefer NOT to catch a fish in a river, rather than NOT to catch a fish in a loch. It can get quite dull just casting into a blank bit of water with nothing ever happening.

THE NORTH COAST

In 1982 I was invited to fish the Dionard by Anthony Duckworth-Chad who had a timeshare on the river. We stayed at the Cape Wrath Hotel, which certainly did not have 5 stars. If you enjoyed overcooked food, especially vegetables, this was your heaven. As an overflow room, the hotel had a static caravan, and one night the incumbent retired to bed only to find the whole floor fell to the ground.

The fishing was interesting as most of the time the water was quite clear as the rain came off rock rather than through peat. One day I was walking up to the top of the river when I spied a pod of salmon moving upstream. From a short distance behind, I followed them, and I can only say that salmon do not run up a river, they walk. It was just a relatively slow and peaceful pace.

I had one particularly interesting encounter with a fish that was showing on a very regular basis. I must have cast a fly in front of it for a good 30 minutes before it took on an extremely aggressive manner and tore off up the pool at a speed so great that the line actually burnt my finger.

In 1990 I took the Kinloch, along with the lodge to celebrate Penny's birthday.

The river was interesting as it was basically a man-made river. If my memory serves me right, it had 54 pools of which only four were natural. We did catch some fish, but it was not only the river that entertained us. I do remember one evening going down to the mouth where the water was quite low, but with an incoming tide, and seeing the salmon entering the river, with some half out of the stream.

When we took the House of Tongue we had a few days on the Borgie. I know that we were blank for the whole fortnight, and I have been to few places where the midges were so bad.

Penny and I went and stayed at Skelpick Lodge on the Naver most years between 1994 and 2004. The big advantage this estate had over the others was that it had the Private Beat, which was between Beat 6 and the Association water. One could have as many rods fishing on the beat as required, whereas the main river had two rods per beat. We were guests of Anthony and Caroline Clegg, and sometimes there would be a third rod.

The lodge was extremely comfortable, big sofas and wide armchairs in the drawing room, but totally unsmart. There was plenty of hot water, a good drying room and plenty of whisky. Finally we were looked after outside by Bob McBain, who was probably the nicest and best ghillie/stalker that I ever have come across. He produced for myself the best day's sport of any kind that I have ever had – more of which later.

The Naver is without doubt a great salmon river, and as in all rivers, when conditions are good, it is fantastic. My experiences were certainly not as many people would expect. On Beat 1, I never caught a fish in either Dal Mallart or Dal Harraild. My first success was in Lower Stables, which would not feature highly in anybody's premier pick of pools, nor would Brown's which I enjoyed fishing. Beat 2 had Syre pool, which had quite fast water at the top, and I remember Bob would always like the rods to strip the line as soon as the fly hit the water. He believed that one could never fish a fly too quickly.

Atmospheric conditions and wind are much discussed as reasons for success or failure in salmon fishing. One morning we were on Beat 5 and

Bob McBain, ghillie and stalker at Skelpick on the River Naver

it was overcast, cool with the wind from the east. The river was dead with nothing showing. Then the wind went away to the west for a brief period of time, and the river came alive. We were fishing the Wall, and I think we caught two or three fish before another change of wind back to the east, and that was it for the rest of the day.

Beat 6 is the best beat that I have fished on any river in Scotland. When it is in good order, two rods would find it difficult to fish every pool properly as there is so much good water. In 1996 we had a strange occurrence when it rained hard but very locally. The top of the river had nothing. Beats 4 to 6 had a good spate. Penny and I were on the main river, the Cleggs were on the Private Beat. Bob McBain put me into the Round Pool, saying, 'A beginner could not fail to catch a fish here today' and took Penny up to the Crooked Stream. Needless to say I touched nothing. I then went to Dal Horrisgle and the action began. I do not remember how many fish I hooked but I landed four, and enjoyed every minute. I ended the morning in the Rock and caught one more. Penny ended up with three on the bank, and we returned to the lodge for a large gin and tonic. The Cleggs had caught eight fish on the Private Beat and so we had 16 salmon for the morning.

The last river on the north coast that I have fished is the Halladale. I first went there in 1980, and we stayed in the Forsinard Hotel. I was with the Duckworth-Chad family and, with the children being quite young, the fishing was not taken that seriously, but we did catch a few salmon.

About 30 years later, I met Patrick Hungerford, who, with three others, had bought the river, top to bottom. He invited me to fish during the first week of July

Dal Horrisgle, Beat 6 on the River Naver

2011. The catch for the whole river for that week was two fish, which were both caught by myself. There was very, very little water in the river, so I spent a lot of time fishing the tidal pools. One could see shoals of salmon entering the river and I would cast a fly in front, and then strip as fast as possible. I had one particularly exciting time when I tied on a bonefish fly called a Crazy Pink Charlie. I cast out and stripped, and a salmon left the shoal following the fly, and then suddenly turned and swam back to join the other fish. It certainly got my heart beating.

The Halladale is a genuine Highland spate river. When there is a spate the river comes alive, and little pools appear between the bigger ones. As the water falls, a number of long stretches of slack come into play, so a good deal of time is spent backing-up. This is not one of my favourite ways of fishing, but maybe I am not very good at it. At the top end of the Halladale it is joined by the Dyke, which tends to be fished towards the back-end. It is small, and extremely exciting when the rains come. I found that I had great success with my own Strawberry Mackenzie fly when casting into coloured water.

After Patrick Hungerford and Toby Ward bought the Halladale they did up Bighouse, which is a large and comfortable lodge. Along with the fishing they have developed a partridge shoot up the river, which, in September, adds much variety to the sporting week.

THE EAST COAST

In 1969 I was invited by Reggie and Lena Palmer, who were friends of my parents, to fish the Helmsdale in June. They had an estate called Latheronwheel some 20 miles north of the river. On the first day, I remember being put into a pool, and catching a good fish almost straightaway. After that I did not touch another thing and saw very few salmon for the rest of the week.

The Brora is another great medium-sized river and I have written about it elsewhere. The tributary flowing past Balnacoil is the Blackwater which carries the bulk of the salmon.

When we took Uppat, we had the fishing on the south coast of the lower Brora. On some days we had as our ghillie Willie Gunn, after whom the famous salmon fly was named. I remember him as a quiet gentle man.

In 1974, Colin Campbell Golding and I went to the Oykel in May. There had been a long period of dry weather, so when we arrived and the heavens opened, we were more than happy. The next morning, with the river in good condition, I was on the Langwell Pool, and hooked a good fish about halfway down. Whilst playing it, I felt the reel was becoming detached from the bar that held it to the rod. Eventually, the two bits parted and I had to play the fish by hand-lining. I did manage to beach it, but as I did, the fly came out of its mouth. In those days, I always carried a gaff and I used it to good effect. George Ross later said, with a grin on his face, that, as the fly was not attached to the salmon, I was technically poaching!

In my opinion the Oykel comes into the same bracket as the Naver, Helmsdale and Brora. When in good order some of the pools are big enough to fish two rods, but there will always be smaller ones that can produce a fish. The river is split into the upper and lower sections, the divide is at the Oykel Bridge. We occasionally had a rod on the two beats, but mainly we took a beat on the lower river. There were three rods per beat and invariably Beat 3 was the most prolific with Langwell being the best pool. One day I asked our team if anybody would like to join me in a pre-breakfast visit to Langwell, on the understanding that we could catch a fish per rod, so as not to upset the rest of the party. We were all successful in 20 minutes and were back fairly promptly.

George Ross was the head ghillie, and I believe rose to that position in his late teens. One of the others was called Alec who moved onto the Dee, I believe, where the graphite rod that he was carrying hit an electric cable and he was killed.

The Einig river's bottom pools came with Beat 1 and I had many interesting times in the falls pool without ever being successful.

The Carron and Braelangwell I have written about elsewhere, but I had an interesting day on the Blackwater when I was driven seven miles up the strath to a shepherd's cottage. I fished all the way down to Croik without any success, but what fun it was to pick and choose each small pot or pool. Just upstream from Croik Farm is a small falls pool which usually holds fish. My brother Alexander and I met a few locals one day returning from fishing the falls pool, and I enquired whether they had any luck. The reply was, 'not very good, just five'. We wondered what a good day produced.

One event in 1984 that was a novel experience was fishing early in the morning on the Kyle of Sutherland. It features in the book *The Salmon Rivers of Scotland* by D. H. Mills and Neil Graesser and every salmon destined for the Carron, Oykel, Einig, Cassley and Shin, would have to swim under Bonar Bridge. We fished from the south bank just upstream of the bridge. We were met by a local who smelt of several distilleries and advised the fly should be Hot Orange. Out came the General Practitioner and I fished the ebb tide, which went at a good speed. The local anglers were casting all sorts of lures from the north bank, but I think that I was the only person to catch a fish whilst I was there.

When we were at Braelangwell one year I took a day's fishing on the top beat of the Beauly, which is where the Glass and the Farrar join up. The team of fishers were Penny and I, Julian and Mafra Smithers and Colin and Liz Campbell Golding. No one was successful.

When we were staying at Farr, I was invited to have a day on the Nairn. I do not remember which beat that I was on, but it was just east of the A9. I took both of my brothers, and during the morning, I hooked a salmon and whilst I was playing it, the reel came away from the rod and fell into the river. Alexander picked it up and I played it by hand-lining. William netted it eventually and it was a fine 3lb grilse.

The first time that I fished the Findhorn was when I was staying at Glenmazeran in September 1973. After shooting one day, I went down to the river with Duncan Davidson, the Head Keeper, and asked if many fish were caught each year. The next second a salmon took my Shrimp fly, and so ended a great day. I next went to the river 25 years later with Anthony Duckworth-Chad who had taken one of the Moy beats. I managed to get one in the pool Mary Rose and the following year I caught a couple more, both also from the same pool.

I first went to the Spey in 1981 with Richard Wellesley, his father and a friend, and Toby Weller-Poley. We were fishing at Ballindalloch and stayed in the castle which was quite close to the river. We did not do very well with the salmon, but we caught about 50 sea trout, mostly during the evening and after dark. The majority came out of the Junction Pool, which could house three rods on it at the same time. The Duke and his friend normally retired to the castle at about 11pm, and then the three of us would rotate on the Junction Pool. The only sound that you could hear, once it was dark, was the flowing river. That was until a sea trout took a fly and then came the sound of a screaming reel. On occasions, the noise of the reel was followed by a silence then a voice would shout 'f—k' as the fish got off.

On thing that I do remember about the Ballindalloch beat was the wading in the bottom two pools, Sawmill and Battery, which were without doubt the worst that I have ever encountered.

In 1994 we joined a party at Arndilly. The river was some feet above best level and therefore I used a spinner, catching a fish in the Long Pool. I am not a great

A mornings catch at Arndilly, River Spey

fan of spinning as one does not get the same feel when playing a fish. However, I would rather catch something on a spinner than not catch a salmon. We went again that year, as I took three days in a charity auction. The rest of the rods were Michael Hollingbery's guests who were a somewhat mixed lot of people. However, 34 grilse were caught whilst we were there.

The following year, I suggested to Jeremy Delmar-Morgan, who was Senior Partner of the stockbrokers that I then worked for, that it would be a good idea to invite some clients to fish. We took the Phones beat at Knockando, which fished three rods. We agreed with Sandy Smith, the ghillie, that we would fish in the morning, have a sleep in the afternoon followed by an early supper, and return to the river at about 7.30pm and fish for salmon until dark, then change rods to fish for sea trout. The object of the week was to put the clients in a pool, get them a fish, and make them happy. The first week that we went there, we managed to catch six fish, but I got all of them, marginally embarrassing!

We took Phones for about ten years and caught some wonderful summer salmon with most being somewhere between 10lb and 18lb. There were also some spectacular evenings fishing for sea trout, more of which elsewhere. Sandy Smith was a very enthusiastic ghillie, and would always stay out with us until late into the night.

I have fished other beats on the Spey which include Knockando, Lower Pitcroy, Gordon Castle, Castle Grant No 1, Tulcan No 3 and Carron and Laggan.

Penny and I went to the Deveron a couple of times and fished the Forglen beat. The beat ran through farming country so when there was a spate, it became quite dirty. We did catch some fish, but being in September they tended to be stale, however they were reasonably sized salmon of up to 18lb. Mark Wrigley took the fishing and usually there was one other rod.

In 1967 James Flower was given a week's fishing on the Dee on the Dinnet beat. I remember very little about it, other than catching a fresh 18lb fish, and the ghillie that looked after us. He was without doubt one of the dourest men that I have ever met. I do not recall his name, but his nickname was Creeping Death.

The South Esk is a charming river and the Kinnaird beat has a reputation for catching big fish, and many years ago, Jeremy Delmar-Morgan and I took it in the early spring of 1993 and 1994. In the latter year, I caught the best looking fish of my life, which weighed just over 18lb and was beautifully formed. We also caught that day a fish of 15lb, but mine was shorter and much deeper. I took countless photographs of it, and much looked forward to framing one. Alas I had failed to put a film in the camera.

The Tay system has been the least successful collection of rivers that I have fished in Scotland. I have not caught a single fish on the Tay, Tummel or Tilt. When staying at Clunes with David Barnett, those staying at the lodge had the right to fish the Garry on the Castle water. One was always fishing for stale fish as it was

SALMON FISHING IN SCOTLAND

Anthony Clegg at Tuchan on the Spey

C.F.vS with two good summer salmon

Doors Pool on Lower Makerstoun, Tweed

August, and therefore there was a requirement for a spate the day before we went to the river. On the 21st August 2008, we were on the hill walking up grouse and in the afternoon it rained so hard that on return to the lodge I was soaked from top to bottom. The next day the Garry was in perfect order, and I caught my first and second salmon, and lost another. That was after 41 years of endeavour, and I have never caught another.

The final river on the East Coast is the Tweed. The beats that I have fished are Upper Pavilion, Upper and Middle Mertoun, Upper and Lower Makerstoun, Upper and Lower Floors, Sprouston, Hendersyde, South Walk, Lower North Walk, The Lees, Birgham Dub and Carham.

The two Mertoun beats are those that I know best, and I have caught a lot of fish on both. Besides salmon and grilse I have caught quite a lot of sea trout, and one year I managed to get three which weighed 6lb, 8lb and 10lb. Middle Mertoun is one of my favourite beats on any river, as most pools are good for holding fish. The top pool, Webbs, is wide and has great wading, and fishes somewhat faster that it looks. This is followed by The Craig, which is complicated at the top with a backwater, and then has a deep run under a rock face where fish show, but I found them difficult to hook. The tail under the far bank is a good spot, but requires a long wade to get there.

SALMON FISHING IN SCOTLAND

My first success on the River Garry after 41 years of endeavour

Angie Delahooke fishing the House Stream on Middle Mertoun, Tweed

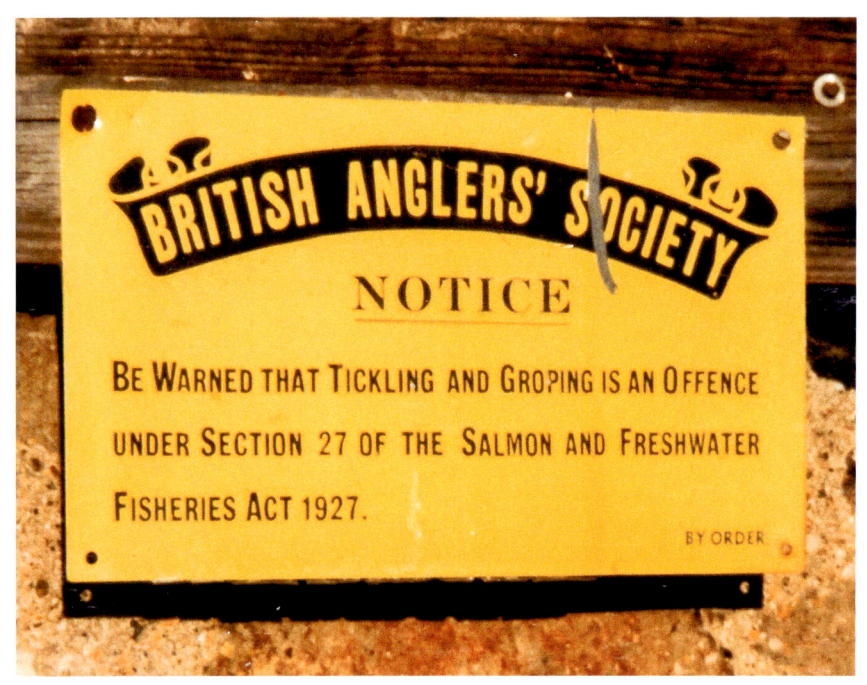

Notice at Upper Mertoun, Tweed

The Bridge Pool seems to be more prolific at the back end. It is a classic looking pool with a long run at the top, a big middle section under the bridge, which fishes best from a boat. The House Stream is very productive, and fish tend to lie above and below the large stone-built point on the far bank. Further down the fish will be in the middle of the river opposite the hut. It is worth fishing all the way down to Willow Bush, but it is best fished by boat on the left bank, or wading on the right bank.

Finally, you come to Collarhaugh, which, in my opinion, is the best pool on any salmon river that I have ever fished. It fishes from top to bottom, and you can hook a fish at any point all the way down. There is a hot spot at the top, off the groin, but there is a shelf on the right side of the pool, and when a fly is placed the far side of the stream, and then comes across the salmon lying below the shelf, they will see it and come up and grab it. The flow of water seems to be very consistent in high and low conditions, so your chances of hooking a fish are good whatever the height.

I have caught quite a lot of fish in Collarhaugh, but my best experience was in July 2016, when I caught in three days, five salmon, all weighing between 10lb and 14lb. The icing on the cake was that every one was taken on my own fly, the Strawberry Mackenzie.

C.F.vS 13lbs and Roger Tyrer 15lbs at Makerstoun, Tweed

I was asked by Hew Blair to fish his bit of the Leader, a tributary of the Tweed. The river was in good order, and in one pool I hooked what I thought was a good fish. It did not move much from the spot where I hooked it but it was fun to play. After a while, I decided to put a bit of pressure on it and I was amazed when a large bit of wood came to the surface. I was somewhat disappointed, but quite amused.

SALMON FISHING IN ICELAND

My first visit to Iceland was in 1997 when I was invited by David Harvey to join a party of his friends and the Velge family from Belgium. We were fishing the Kjarra, which is the top half of one river divided into two, the bottom half being the Thvera. The drive from the airport to the river took many hours as the tunnel under one of the fjords had not been built then, but it was more than interesting looking at the countryside. There was mile upon mile of bare lava rock with practically no trees, but acres of wild lupins. The farms by the coast were mainly grasslands, with a lot of ponies, some sheep and almost no cows. It was a relief to get to the lodge and have a view of the river with its gin-clear water.

We fished a different beat each day so I had no chance to get to know the river, but the pools tended to be small to medium in size with plenty of fast water. I caught one fish each day, which was fine, but perhaps I expected more. Two incidents remain in my mind. I used a single-handed rod of 9 ft, and hooked a fish which played well for a while and then took off downstream to the next pool, followed by the next pool, and then continued on down to the fourth pool. I thought that I must have a decent fish on the end of my line because I never saw it during the time that I was playing it. Finally the fish gave up the fight and I beached it. I was amazed to see that it was probably just 4lb!

The second thing of interest that happened was when David Harvey and I went

Rettarhylur on River Kjarra

far up the river to a good pool called Lower Red Rock. I was fishing with Micro fly, which was a tiny little thing, and I caught a fish. David went into the same pool and put on a 3-inch Collie Dog and immediately hooked and landed a fish. In my life as a fisherman I have heard hundreds of people pontificate about size and colour of salmon flies. I think this experience probably shows that nobody has a clue why salmon take different flies.

A few years later, the stockbrokers I worked for, Teather and Greenwood, were taken over by the Icelandic bank, Landsbanki. It did not take me long to ascertain that one of the two Chief Executives was a keen fisherman, and I told him that it would be a fantastic way to entertain clients if I could take them to one of the Icelandic salmon rivers. A group of people from the office were invited by the bank to go and fish the river Kjos on the west coast. This was in late July and early August for the next two years. If you were on the right beat it was extremely exciting, but there were some quite quiet bits in the middle of the river.

The following years we went to a new river, the Langa. This was altogether a different experience. The river was divided into three beats with each beat divided again into two. There were two rods on each half beat, which meant that one had three hours on each half beat before moving downstream. When we arrived at the lodge, a young man came up to me and asked if he could ghillie for me. His name was Tim Edwards and he had been at Harrow with my nephews. His family had fished the river for many years, and so he knew the pools extremely well.

There are nearly 100 pools in the river, with the best being in the bottom half. Most of them are quite small compared to Scottish rivers, and so a 9ft rod was big enough to cover most of the water. The river enters the sea via a waterfall which varies in height in accordance with the tide. At high tide, the fish can swim straight in, and at low tide they cannot get up the falls. I did on occasions fish into the sea, and caught a few using two tubes together on the end of the line. I had to walk the hooked fish round the headland so that the ghillie could find somewhere to land it. There are three small pools just above the falls, which are called Last Hope, Last Hole and Crocodile. I had a great time one year when I hooked four fish in quick succession in Crocodile, and landed two of them, whilst the other two turned tail and swam through the next two downstream pools, over the falls and out to sea, becoming detached in the process. A little further upstream was the Foss Pool, which was always a great place to hitch a fly across the top of the water. There were two vital rules to be followed – never stop stripping the fly and do not strike when a salmon rises.

All the pools were numbered but there is one that is unique, and has the number 31½. The story that I heard about the pool was one of the regular rods on the river was Michael Heathcoat-Amory who had a man called Barry who looked after him when he was fishing. Barry apparently found this pool, which is a small run under the far bank, which broadens out at the bottom. Fish were obviously caught in it

TALES OF MOOR AND STREAM

and it became one of the most prolific pools on the whole river. Its name is Barry's Pond. Other pools of note were Daredevil and Harlequin, which you could fish from many different angles.

Barry's Pond on River Langa

The first salmon to be caught in Iceland with a Strawberry Mackenzie

In 2011, I shared a beat on the Langa with Toby Ward, and one morning he played a practical joke on me that still brings a smile to my face when I think about it. He had had a successful morning and I had struggled to land a fish, but we planned to meet at Barry's Pond before returning to the lodge for lunch. I was being driven down the river by the ghillie and I could see Toby kneeling by the river, and looking as if he was returning a fish back into the water. When we were about 100 yards from him, I saw a splash just in front of the kneeling figure and assumed the salmon's tail had slapped the water as it swam away. I thought to myself, 'Lucky so-and-so'. When I got out of the car, I said something like 'Not another one?' Toby replied, 'No, but I thought that I would wind you up, so I knelt by the pool as if I was putting a fish back, and smacked the water with my hand to create the splash.' I was had, hook, line and sinker!

In 2008 I had my first visit to the Haffjardara river. A good friend of mine, Bo Ivanovic, had a half share in the river and asked me if I would like to spend a couple of days with him, after my stay on the Langa. In fact it turned out that I would have two half days there, but I still managed to catch seven salmon.

Bo Ivanovic and Buby Calvo in Haffjardara Lodge

I returned to the Haffjardara in 2013 and had four days in June, and then three days in July. Normally, in the month of June, one would expect to catch more salmon than grilse, but of the 16 fish that I landed, 11 were grilse. When I returned

Mark Cannon-Brookes fishing Falls Pool on the Haffjardara

in July the river was in great order and full of fresh grilse. The first half day was good and I got three fish, but what followed on the next two days was exceptional. During the first full day I hooked and landed 10 grilse, with the next day being nearly the same, i.e. nine grilse. The final half day I got four fish in the tail of the Sheep Pool. One interesting fact of that trip was that I hooked 26 salmon, and landed all of them.

There are so many attributes that are attached to being able to fish the Haffjardara. The lodge is very comfortable and in a ideal position, being about halfway up the river. There are three beats with two rods per beat, and it is quite a short river, so it does not take more than 15 to 20 minutes to drive to the furthest pool.

In my opinion, the fact that the Haffjardara scores so highly is that it doesn't have good or bad beats. The most productive pool is Sheep, but every beat has a number of good pools, and some are not easy to fish. The Falls Pool, Kvorn, is extremely tricky, sometimes frustrating, but always exciting. I thoroughly enjoy Aquarium at the top of the river, and also Broken Bank, which is much like Barry's Pond on the Langa. Others worth a mention are Kula, Dick's, Bakki and the Old Bridge.

One of the biggest pleasures of going to the Haffjardara was the presence of the head ghillie, Ingi. He was always very enthusiastic, but calm in the way he approached any action on the river. He was brilliant at seeing fish lying in the pools, and so he could direct you to any part of a pool. As most ghillies did in

Iceland, he would change flies all the time, going from micro hitches to Snaeldas and Sunray Shadows. One thing that I shall not forget was his vehicle – the oldest, dark blue, long-wheelbase Land Rover.

In 2014, and for the next two years, a team of seven, which included David Harvey, David Barnett, Michael Barclay and Seton Wills, went to the Kjarra. We did not catch as many fish as expected but one or two pools like Runki, Colonel's Vigholskvora and Rettarhylur were memorable. I had two ghillies who looked after me extremely well. The first year my guide was Toggi, who was mad keen on fishing

C.F.vS and Toggi on the Kjarra

C.F.vS at Aquarium, Haffjardara

Thor with my fish from Kula on the Haffjardara

Eric Koberling on the Kjarra

and knew the river well. When he was not on the riverbank, he was a Police Chief Inspector. For the next two years I was lucky to have Erik Koberling, a young German who was at university in Holland. He was a fishing fanatic, and tended to my every need on the riverbank. He was thrilled whenever I hooked a salmon, and was a great help when I was wading.

The following years I put together a small team which included Richard Bernays, David Barnett and Nick Wingfield-Digby. We went firstly to the Midfjardara, a river with a reputation for

SALMON FISHING IN ICELAND

David Barnett at Runki, Kjarra

big catches, but the water level was very low and that precluded our fishing on a number of pools. For the first time, I found the ghillies and the staff in the lodge not particularly friendly and not that enthusiastic. We caught fish, but I cannot remember any of the pools nor any of the salmon that I hooked. We travelled on to the Dolum, a much smaller river which was also lacking water. The only thing that happened of interest to myself was that I hooked seven fish and lost the lot! I returned to the Midfjardara the following year and there was considerably more water, so I fished more pools and caught more fish. I had an American, Jason, as my ghillie who never let me choose my own flies and was quite dictatorial.

In 2019 I decided to change rivers and I took the whole of the Grimsa for the first four days of the season. Six of us fished four rods. It was all a bit disappointing as the river was low and there were few fish about. We caught 20 fish, of which I was lucky enough to get five salmon and two grilse. The salmon averaged 14lb in weight.

Ptarmigan on the banks of the Grimsa

Arctic Tern chick

45

Icelandic dinner, first course (clockwise from top left) reindeer, puffin, guillemot, reindeer sausage, seal, gannet and cormorant

GROUSE SHOOTING – ENGLAND

I shot my first grouse in 1959 and since then I have shot on 43 different moors or hills, of which 18 are in England, and 35 are in Scotland.

The first venture was on a small moor called Thornton which is a short distance from the village of Aysgarth in Wensleydale. We had a day's walking up and got 7 brace, and three days later we went there again and I got my first grouse. During that day, a flock of birds flew over me, and my father shouted 'Have a go at them'. I fired two shots, certainly without taking aim, and killed two golden plovers! That was my first right and left. But sadly only one was picked. I remember it tasted delicious.

About a couple of days later my father and uncle and I were invited to Howden Lodge, a small moor adjoining Melmerby and owned in those days, I think, by Colonel Ferrand. The drives were all quite short and I remember we shot one drive three times in the day – the first drive, the last before lunch, and the last of the day. We got 15½ brace, and I shot my first driven grouse. I was lucky enough to be able to shoot there quite a few times over the following years.

A couple of years later, I was invited to shoot on Caldbergh, which was owned or taken by three families, the Harrison-Tophams, the Chadwyck-Healeys and the Craven-Smith-Milnes. I remember on one occasion, the last drive of the day was on a slope, and I was in the top butt with a reasonable view of the whole drive. Coveys started to get up and as they flew other coveys rose to join them. In the end most birds were airborne at the same time, and when they came to the guns, they covered the whole line.

Two days later I want to Scrafton, which is next to Caldbergh. In one drive I was number seven and was not expecting much to come my way. However, an enormous pack of grouse came over, and I fired my right and left barrels, and then reloaded three times into the same lot. I have always wondered how many grouse were in that pack. I remember that I shot three birds.

That same year my uncle took Marske in Swaledale on a long lease. He paid £50 a year for 25 years, and his other costs were practically nothing as there were no keepers and what heather burning that was needed to be done, was executed by the two farmers who owned the moor. The beaters' pay was usually covered by the sale of the grouse.

The size of the moor was roughly 400 acres and initially we did two drives in the morning, had lunch and then did the same drives in the afternoon. Latterly I was allowed to change the format so that we had three drives in the morning and two in the afternoon, and the birds were driven to different lines of butts. I experimented with one new line and it was very successful, so much so that John Allison, one of the farmers, banned it, as he thought that we would shoot too many birds.

The moor was shot about four times a year, and the bag was usually between 20 and 40 brace. The record was 77 brace, which is amazing when it was from such a small acreage.

A week later, I had two days on a moor called Melmerby, which was close to Scrafton and Caldbergh, but I think a bit smaller. So, in the space of ten days and at the age of 17, I had six days' driven grouse shooting. The only other moor that I had a day on at that stage in my life was Coverhead, which was towards the top of Coverdale. The only thing that I recall was that the day of 8½ brace was the smallest in living memory.

For something like 20 years, a team of us including David Harvey, George West, Piers Brooke, Anthony Duckworth-Chad, Sam and Mark Vestey, Philip Chetwode and others, took Castle Bolton moors for three days at the end of August. The two higher moors Apedale and West Moor were the better beats, but the Low Moor was useful if the cloud was down. We would shoot between 75 and 150 brace each day and we paid the same rent whatever the bag. Eventually we were asked to pay for what we shot and the consensus said No!

On one occasion some of the guns shooting at Castle Bolton and I went and had

Philip Chetwode and Anthony Duckworth-Chad at Bolton Castle

a day at Mossdale, near Hawes. The moor was owned by the van Cutsems, and I remember having breakfast or lunch in a pub at Buttertubs with the only others eating there being a man and a woman who did not seem to fit in. I later found out that they were both police officers looking after Prince William.

The first time that I shot at Middlesmoor was supposed to be two days with a team put together by Colin Campbell Golding. We had one drive and then the cloud came down and that was the end of proceedings. We drove off on the third day in bright sunshine. However, in 1988, I was invited back, and we shot on a beat that I think was called High West. The days consisted of two drives in the morning, being a drive and return, then lunch, and exactly the same in the afternoon. I remember the last drive well as I was one away from being the end gun on the right of the line. All the birds that came to myself and the gun on my right flew from left to right. At the end of the drive we were asked by the pickers-up how many birds did the two of us think that we had shot. We both said 21, giving a total of 42. They picked 48. None of the birds could have been shot by the other guns. The bag for the day was 250 brace.

I also had days in that area at Stean, Bolton Abbey, Conistone, Grassington and further south in Derbyshire at Crag. The two things that remain in my memory about our stay at Crag was, firstly, on arrival, being greeted by three members of the staff, a butler and two footmen, to take our luggage. The second was one of the lunches that we had, which consisted of the biggest collection of cold food that I have ever seen on a table. There was every sort of cold meat, pies, hams, chickens, pâtés and a whole ox tongue.

Finally I must include probably my worst experience on a grouse moor. My brother had taken a day on East Arkengarthdale, which now includes our old stamping ground Marske. It was a misty day and we arrived a bit late, as no one knew where to go. The head keeper was not amused at our tardiness. At the end of the second drive and after the whistle had been blown to indicate no more shooting in front, a snipe got up and the beaters shouted 'Snipe!'. The bird flew straight upwards and unfortunately my other brother, Alexander, fired at it. The bird was high above the beaters' heads, but it was in front. The head keeper stormed up to Alexander and let fly, with every other word beginning with the letter 'f'. At lunch there was a major row between guns and the head keeper, after which there was a stand-off. I voted that no one should give him a tip, but I was over-ruled. We were asked if we would like another day and everyone said 'No!'.

GROUSE SHOOTING – SCOTLAND

Over a period of 55 years I went to 25 estates in Scotland to shoot grouse. The vast majority of the days were walking up, some of those were shooting over dogs which I always enjoyed. I marvelled at the elegance of setters quartering the hill, and in most cases, how steady they were at the point.

A few years after our three week stay at Balnacoil. I was invited to stay at Gordonbush by Jessie Tyser. We shot every day for a week, and there were a lot of grouse that year which was 1969. My game book shows that we got over 250

Farr House Party. Margaret Mogg, Nan Danby, A.deL.vS, John Mogg, Denys Danby, W.H.vS, C.F.vS, H.H.vS, Philip Flower, A.H.vS

George, the grouse between Farr and Glenkyllachy

brace in the six days. The other guns were mostly young, except for Jim Pilkington who was an extremely kind and charming person. I was invited again the following year, and that included shooting on the neighbouring estate, Kintradwell, which the Tysers also owned. Unfortunately, a tragedy happened on the hill one day, when Jim Pilkington's dog, Wigeon, was shot by one of the guns. We were not invited again.

One of the estates that we went to early in my life was Farr, which was just south of Inverness. It marched with Glenkyllachy which was also owned by Colin Mackenzie. We shot most days on Farr, but occasionally the two estates were used for a day's driven grouse shooting. There was a road across the hill, which went from the lodge on Farr to the lodge on Glenkyllachy. At some high point there lived a single cock grouse who did not appreciate cars or humans invading his territory. When a car arrived in his area, he would fly next to the vehicle shouting his annoyance. Sometimes we would stop and get out. George, that was his name, would advance and if you had a stick he would take it in his beak and flap his wings in anger. The BBC sent a TV crew up to Scotland to film this extraordinary bird.

When I stayed at Clunes, some of the guns would be asked to go and shoot on nearby estates. Dalnamein marches with Clunes and three of us went there on the invitation of Lord Allerton who used to take the estate. I remember going to the hill in the same Land Rover as Lady Allerton and when we got to a gate in the deer fence, I opened the door to open the gate, but I was told in no uncertain terms to say where I was, as she put it – 'The pony boy will do it, that is what he is here for'. I made no comment. We had a good day nevertheless, and the first three birds that got up in front of me were snipe, and I shot all of them. Thereafter I could not miss!

I had quite a few days on the Castle beat at Blair Atholl, which marched with Clunes. The Duke of Atholl always had huge yellow Labradors with names like Brasso and Blotto, which seemed keen to mount any dog, whatever came along. We had one memorable day, right at the back of the estate, in the deepest peat bogs that I have ever seen. This beat had not been shot for a long time, and as it had been very dry you could walk on the peat and did not sink in up to the waist. We had to carry what we shot as ponies would not be able to get through the bogs, and so after having had our piece and decanted the morning's bag, we set off for the afternoon. The day was cut short because we could not carry any more birds, and the bag for the day, for six guns, was 56½ brace.

Five guns staying at Clunes once went to Dalnaspidal and joined Roger Adams' team, making up a line of 11 guns. We had a great day and shot 73 brace. One other hill the Barnetts took was Edradour which was north of Pitlochry. The ground was always driven and we could usually shoot between 40 and 50 brace.

The last place that I know that we went to was Riemore. I remember nothing about it at all.

When we fished the Oykel, for the first two years we stayed in a cottage in Ullapool, that was owned by the Troughtons. It was through their introductions that we were able to walk up grouse and ptarmigan on Braemore, Foich and Leckmelm.

C.F.vS at Glanmazeran

GROUSE SHOOTING – SCOTLAND

On September 5, 1972, Anthony Duckworth-Chad, my brother William and I went to Braemore and shot 7½ brace of grouse and 7½ brace of ptarmigan – an amazing day. Two days later we were at Foich, and Anthony shot the highest grouse that I have ever seen killed. It must have been put up by a raptor, but it was an exceptional shot.

Some years later when fishing the Oykel, we stayed at the Oykel Bridge Hotel, and/or Craggie Cottage, which was just up the road from the hotel. We had the odd day's shooting close by on Loubcroy and Duchally.

When we stayed at Uppat and had the fishing on the south bank of the Brora, we also had the shooting, on some days, at Uppat and Dunrobin. We had a couple of days when we shot about 20 brace. The owner of Uppat also had an estate on the north coast called Tongue, which we went to in 1970. There was the odd grouse on the hill, but not many. While we were there, I was asked for a day at Latheronwheel, just north of Helmsdale, owned by the Palmer family. Again it was a day's walking up for not many birds. We stayed again at Latheronwheel a few years later, and shot a number of wild English partridges.

Three other estates that I had days at were all driven grouse. Invergeldie was owned by the Priestleys, and had one very interesting drive, where a few hundred yards behind the butts, the hill came to an end. The birds flew through the line and when they came to the end of the hill, they turned and flew back, so often the guns had birds coming from both directions. I shot at Dumfries House some years after the time when the hill was full of grouse. Heather beetle and disease left it in a very sorry state, which was sad to see. The final place was Glenmazeran, west of the A9 on the Findhorn. I was staying there with the Elphinstones, and we shot 81 brace, of which 75 brace were shot in the morning. In the afternoon, the midges appeared in great numbers, and I thought that I would light the heather on my butt to create a bit of smoke. A fire took hold, and I had difficulty in extinguishing it – a bit embarrassing.

STALKING

Colin Reid, stalker at Clunes

For many a year, stalking was my favourite sport on the hill. A lot of it could be put down to the fact that there cannot be a bigger difference between driving a desk in a stockbroker's office in London EC2, and walking on a Scottish hill with one other person. It is very noisy in a room with many people on the telephone all day, but the complete silence, except for the wind, of an empty hillside is truly wonderful. Occasionally a cock grouse would rise in front, making its presence felt with a good 'g'back, g'back'. Sadly I never stalked in October, and so I did not hear a stag roar, but certainly I did hear hinds barking in alarm. The only time that I did hear a stag roar was in a zoo in Sydney, Australia!

I spent many an hour sitting in a peat bog, waiting either for the rain to stop or the mist to clear, chatting to the stalker about everything and anything to do with the hill. I learnt a great deal of the dos and don'ts, especially that once you start a day's stalking, the stalker is totally in charge. In my opinion, a day on the hill is always interesting and usually exciting, and if you have a blank day it simply doesn't matter. If one gets a beast, it is the icing on the cake, and if you miss a beast, it is always disappointing. However to wound a stag, and then not find it, is a disaster.

On a day's stalking, it is important to wear the right clothes and carry the correct contents in a shoulder bag. It is probable that you will get wet from above the knee downwards, so that should be taken for granted. A good coat is vital, and towelling for one's neck is well worth taking. Waterproof boots and knee-length gaiters help a great deal.

In my bag, I would put a spare sleeveless jersey, and a pair of gloves, as the temperature at 2,000 feet is always colder than outside the lodge's front door. I never took alcohol to the hill, but a can of beer or a flask can always be put in the vehicle that carries one to where the stalking day begins. Water is always available from the burns and a telescopic cup is useful. A tip that was given to me about drinking from a burn was to quench one's thirst, and then drink the same amount again, and you will not be thirsty for a good while. I would take two baps for my piece with lettuce, and tomatoes for the moisture, but my favourite bap was always fried egg and bacon. Two apples is a good idea, and cheese and biscuits for tea. I also always take sweets or chewing gum to get the juices flowing.

The three main changes during my stalking career were the transport on the hill, the rifles and the communication between the stalker and the ponyman. In the early 1960s the stalker and I walked from where the vehicle that took us to the hill stopped. We would usually meet the ponyman at this pre-arranged place, and he would be told roughly where we would be going. He would be leading a garron, or two. The first tracked vehicle that I remember was a Snow Track. When I was at Gordonbush, Jessie Tyser took, what I was told was, a WWI Citroën half-track to the hill, which was quite heavy, and so got bogged down in the wet peat. Then Argocats began to arrive in the UK and they revolutionised travel over the hill. They could pretty well go anywhere and were great for carrying beasts back to base.

I started stalking in the 1960s and used open sights for a number of years, as it was regarded by some people that putting a telescope on a rifle was somehow making life too easy. Nowadays all rifles have telescopes, and usually have two legs/props at the front for better stability. That certainly helps me, as I sometimes suffer from stag fever.

Before walkie-talkies were invented, communications between stalkers and ponymen was really only by sight, so the ponyman would have to look for signs of where the stalking party might be. Often, I remember, we would light a small fire in the heather, and generally the smoke would be visible and it meant that there was a stag to be collected. Sometimes the beast would have to be dragged to a more amenable position. Somehow we always made contact, but two-way radios now certainly make life on the hill a great deal easier.

I stalked on 18 different estates, and the main difference, in my opinion, was the gradient of the hills. The most difficult was Glen Etive where you were given a particular ridge for the day. I do not remember walking on a bit of even ground, you

The high tops at Glen Etive

either went up or down. We never saw a single beast, but the most spectacular thing that I saw was a bird of prey rising from the bottom of a corrie without a wingbeat for some 2,000 feet in a very short time.

Braemore also had some steep slopes on the side of Beinn Dearg, and I had a memorable stalk on the side of a cliff. The stalker told me to wait for the stag to face uphill because if I shot at it and it ran facing downhill, it would fall a long way down the cliff face. I fired and it turned 180 degrees and ran flat out over the precipice. We did not bother to collect the beast as the stalker said it would be crushed by the fall. One other thing that I remember was getting to the top of a high hill and finding a spring gently flowing, and producing the most delicious cold water.

I had a few days on the hills of Farr and Glenkyllachy. The stalker took me into the woods on the Glenkyllachy side to look for a sika stag on one occasion. It was rather like playing hide and seek, much moving from tree to tree and much use of the binoculars. I did manage to get one, which had a very pretty head.

I went to Glenmazeran when it was owned by the Elphinstones and had some happy days there. Some years later, when it had been bought by the Benyons, a friend took it for the stalking. I had the worst day of my life on the hill. The stalker was bone idle, and we left late in the morning to have a cursory look for a stag, before returning to the woods above the lodge, to await any beast that might return for the night. Eventually one appeared, which I shot, and that was the end of the day. I regretted giving him a tip.

When staying at Clunes in 1969, Anthony Tufton, now Lord Hothfield, and I were invited to stalk at Ben Alder. We drove up the A9 to the lodge north of Loch Ericht and breakfasted with the Byam-Cooks. We then went by boat to the top of the loch, where we were met by the stalker, a ghillie to carry the rifle and a ponyman with two garrons. We stalked back towards the lodge, both of us getting a stag. We arrived at a bothy, next to the sanctuary, which was above the lodge, where refreshments in the form of whisky and Heinz tomato soup were awaiting us. Outside there were three US Army Willys jeeps which ferried us back to the lodge. So ended a great day.

Some years later I had a day on North Drumochter which lies to the south of Loch Ericht. We started from the shore of the loch and slowly walked, and spied our way to the top of Beinn Udlamain, 3,317 feet, about the last 500 feet being all scree, which was difficult to climb, but much worse coming down. I remember when we crested the top, we had to duck down to allow a large pack of ptarmigan

Spying North Dromochter from Ben Alder on the north bank of Loch Ericht

to fly over us. I recall stopping on the way up to watch a Hercules aeroplane, way below us, practising low flying up Loch Ericht. It was so far away I was able to put the aircraft between my thumb and finger.

We stayed at the House of Tongue, on the north coast one year and during one day when we were walking up grouse, we put up a stag which was lying in some tall heather. After lunch I decided to take a rifle to the hill to see if I could find it and have a stalk. I never did encounter it again, and so returned to the lodge. However, when I was reading a book entitled *Outside Days* by Max Hastings, I came upon a story which was almost identical to my adventure, except that his stalk on the same ground was successful. So, on my return to London, I invited him to join me for lunch at White's and we could compare our stories. I received a fairly curt letter, which left me in no doubt that he had no interest in such a meeting.

The only hind that I ever shot was on the Ben More estate on Mull. I was invited there by John Skeffington, whose father owned it, along with Killiechronan. We stayed in Knock House, which was without doubt, the coldest place that I have ever stayed in. There was no central heating, and you had to run from the bathroom to your bedroom before you lost all warmth.

I stalked on Alladale when staying at Braelangwell, and remember one glen going west from the lodge which was one of the prettiest I have ever seen. I did not enjoy the day as it was extremely commercial, and I had to pay extra to use the estate rifle.

Other places that I went to include Kinlochewe, Loubcroy and Applecross, which is on the west coast and owned by the Wills family. I was never allowed a shot as the stalker was afraid that Captain Andrew would be annoyed that I had shot a beast that was too small, or too big, or had too fine a head. Then there was Skelpick on the north coast which is another story – the best day's sport that I ever had.

One large regret that I have is that I never stalked in the rut. I would have much enjoyed seeing stags protecting their hinds and watching other beasts trying to take advantage of hinds that have wandered. I have had many, many days stalking without having had a shot, and thoroughly enjoyed most of them.

DOGS

Having a dog by my side on a day's shooting has been an integral part of my sporting life. The first bitch we owned was a Labrador called Binty. She was definitely a pet rather than a working dog, and when we had a litter, we kept one of the puppies, Becky.

My father was a keen shooting man, but never had a great affinity with dogs, so it was left to me to introduce Becky to the thrills of picking-up. This I did by taking her rough-shooting on the nearby farm where I occasionally got a pheasant or pigeon. As in all sporting dog breeds she had an aptitude to hunt and retrieve, and before long she became extremely keen. She instilled in me the pleasure of having a constant companion on the shooting field.

Becky had an instinct that always amazed me. During the winter months, I would go from London to spend the weekend at home with my parents. On Friday evenings she would wait at the front door for my arrival before dinner, assuming that I would be shooting the next day. I did not prepare my kit until early the following morning, so she was not given any hints, but she would always lie

Becky retrieving at Marske

TALES OF MOOR AND STREAM

Jemima, Juno and Bess

Bonny, after a day's shooting

outside my bedroom door, eager to be off and away. Sunday mornings she was not to be seen.

The next Labrador, Bess, was a character. I do not know if she came with a grand pedigree, but she looked half Labrador and half Greyhound. She was seriously fast and when happy or embarrassed, she would curl her lips upwards, showing all her teeth and look extremely intimidating. However, her demeanour was enchanting, and she was loved by all.

Bess had one litter of puppies from which we retained Jemima, who was a bit on the dull side, but she served one great purpose in my father's sporting life. She thoroughly enjoyed joining him on the banks of the Test at Longparish, and watching him catch many a good trout. She also had puppies and we kept Juno who was one of the sweetest dogs that I have ever known. She was the only dog that I have seen walk through the front door of Pynkney Hall, home of the Duckworth-Chads and was allowed to lie in the corner of the dining-room.

Some of the happiest memories of my entire sporting life are picking up with Bess, Jemima and Juno at Hambleden near Henley, and having all dogs

Mimi

Bumble and Tally

working well at the same time. It was lovely to watch, and made me feel quite proud.

Soon after I got married to Penny, she acquired a black Labrador puppy which I named Bonny. She was quite small, but very active, and after a short period away being trained, she turned into a fine shooting companion.

Mimi followed, and she had a very sweet nature, and she also was an extremely keen picker-up. A lot of my shooting involved walking up grouse in Perthshire and all of my dogs behaved pretty well on the hill.

My current shooting friend, Bumble, may not be perfect on all shooting days, but I have never wanted a dog that only did what it was told and did not think for

Mimi and her puppies

itself. Many a fine retrieve has she completed in her life and enjoyed every minute. One attribute she has had, and self-taught, was the ability to point when walking up grouse. It was wonderful to watch and certainly gave me more shooting than the other guns. Sadly, her sporting days are over.

THE BEST DAY'S SPORT OF MY LIFE

An invitation to fish one of the finest salmon rivers in the north of Scotland in September 1994 was received, and readily accepted. For week upon week the sun had shone and spates were remembered as something of the past. The second week of the month was no exception, and we were lucky to have caught six rather stale fish by Friday. Four of these came from one pool on Wednesday morning when the wind changed from the north-east to the west. There was intense activity for two hours, and the one fish that I caught, I had risen seven times before it took hold.

The owner of the property, on hearing of our struggle, kindly offered a day's stalking in recompense, and I was asked if I would like a day on the hill. The answer was immediate, and in the affirmative. Bob McBain, the stalker, and I drove for some 45 minutes to the far end of the estate, unloaded the Argocat, and set off to the first spy point. It was noticeable how much cooler it was on the tops, and the rain started to fall in earnest. We spied shootable stags to the north and another bunch farther away to the south-east.

Bob decided that we would try to get a beast from the lot in the north as the wind was favourable. Despite disturbing a hind which lay hidden from our view until we were not 20 yards from her, we had a relatively easy stalk into the stags. Bob selected one for me to shoot, but suddenly a hummel appeared from behind a knoll, and my aim changed. I thought my shot was good, but they all galloped away round the shoulder and my heart sank. We collected our sticks and rifle case and set off to see what had happened. As we rounded the hill we saw the stag lying dead not 100 yards from where he had been. Having completed the gralloch we walked to the nearest point from which we could see if the shot had disturbed the beasts to the south. The answer was no, and so eating our piece on the move, we started on our second stalk of the day.

The rain was relentless, and it was beginning to shift the deer from where they were lying. We had two fruitless stalks, and the herd started to move away towards a re-seed where they would spend the night. It was now decision time. There was the hummel two miles away, waiting to be collected, and the second lot were moving in the opposite direction. Bob then amazed me with his suggestion which was for him to collect the stag and for me to stalk on my own. I felt that I had been awarded my school colours.

Taking the rifle, I set off on a parallel line to the herd which was about half a mile to the left. The first few hundred yards was an easy walk downhill, but then I found myself in open ground and in full view. In front there was boggy ground with reeds which would provide good cover, and so I started a long crawl towards a deep burn. Constantly I checked on the stags' whereabouts and their general disposition. Suddenly they were all alert and looking about themselves. The reason was soon obvious – startled sheep. A dark object crawling through reeds was definitely a worry to them. I stayed put, getting drenched from below as well as above, until both deer and sheep relaxed.

Before continuing down into the burn I looked for a cross reference on the far side which hopefully would be opposite the beasts when I started the final approach. At no time was the wind a problem, only the sheep. It was rather like grandmother's footsteps; move until they moved and then stop and wait. My progress was painfully slow and I was afraid my assumption of where the stags were would be totally wrong. Eventually I climbed out of the burn and made my way forwards to my chosen knoll. On approaching the crest I suddenly saw antlers not 40 yards away from me. I dropped to the ground like a stone and waited. Slowly, I eased myself up to see where they were and the antlers had disappeared. I fortunately made the assumption that they were moving slowly towards the re-seed and made my way back down the hill so as to stalk them from a different angle. I took the rifle out of its case and crawled towards what I hoped would be an appropriate firing position. On arrival there was the herd moving diagonally away from me, not disturbed, but purposely walking onwards. What was I to do – make a noise to attract their attention or hope that a shootable beast would stop and stand still. Almost immediately a heavy-topped stag stopped and I had no alternative but to aim and fire. It dropped where it had stood. I reloaded and prayed it would not jump up and run. There was no movement after a couple of minutes, so I slowly approached it, making sure I was downhill. The stag was dead and my worries abated.

I waited for about an hour for Bob to return and we met at our rendezvous. I was soaked but elated. When weighed the hummel scaled 14st 2lb, and the other was an 11 pointer turning 18st 8lb. People talk of red letter days – I doubt that I will ever have a better day on the hill.

A LIST OF OUTSTANDING DAYS

The best day's sport that I ever had was a day's stalking at Skelpick, in the north of Scotland. The head stalker was Bob McBain – one of the most likeable and able men that I have ever met on the hill and on the river.

The most thrilling and exciting experience in my fishing life was about an hour and a half on the Phones beat at Knockando on the Spey. The fish that we, as a team, were after, were sea trout.

Sandy Smith fishing the Pouches on the Phones Beat at Knockando, where I had the best hour and half of my fishing life.

The unsung hero of many Scottish salmon rivers is the sea trout. It is a truly magnificent floating fish and wins hands down in the contest against its better-known opponent.

Some years ago I had taken a middle beat on the Spey in early June. The weather was warm and a bit on the bright side. So, on the advice of our ghillie, Sandy Smith, we divided the day into three parts. The morning session took us through to lunch, which sometimes started quite early, was usually protracted and certainly not teetotal. We then returned to our lodgings for a serious siesta. Dinner was taken early so that we were back on the river by 8pm and fishing for salmon until about 11pm. We changed to lighter, single-handed rods to fish for sea trout.

On one of the evenings, I was allocated a fantastic pool, the Pouches, that had a long, fast stream at the head with calmer water on either side. After about 100 yards the pool turned sharply to the left and widened out for a similar distance. Sandy's advice was to walk a hooked fish round the corner and land it in the calm, deep water. I went to the top of the run, descended some steps and waded out a few paces.

Casting a line when it is dark is a different experience to fishing during the day. I felt that my cast was too long or too short and that my line was often in a tangle, so much time was spent checking the fly. However, after a relatively short period, I hooked a fish, which took off into the pool. It was airborne a lot of the time and I had no idea where it was until I managed to get some semblance of control.

So as not to disturb the rest of the pool, I made my way back to the bank and played the sea trout from dry ground, slowly edging downstream, round the corner, where I beached it.

I went back to the fishing hut to check that the fly, a Silver Stoat's Tail, was still firmly attached to the line, and returned to the head of the pool and started downstream again. It did not take long before I was playing fish number two, which disappeared into the dark yonder, giving me another thrilling fight.

In the next hour or so, I repeated the process a further seven times and I never got to the bottom of the pool without hooking a fish. I lost four of the nine fish that I had hooked but that is par for the course. I did change my fly to a Blue Elver, which was very successful. The sea trout weighed 4lb to 5lb and were all fresh from the sea but without sealice.

The other two rods had caught few fish themselves, but I was the lucky one. That piscatorial adventure was, without doubt, the most exciting two hours that I have spent on any river.

A Special Day's Partridge Shooting

I had to wait until I was 73 years old before I experienced my best day's shooting. This happened at Laverstoke, near Whitchurch, in Hampshire. We were shooting partridges in October, and the landscape is very much laid out for what I would call 'old-fashioned' partridge shooting. The guns stand not far back from high hedges, which means that the birds are over you fairly quickly, so the routine is to raise one's gun, swing and fire.

On this particular shoot I like to have the opportunity of shooting with two guns, mainly so that I do not have to worry about all my kit at the end of the drive, and then I can pick up at leisure with my dog. Jeremy is my usual loader who gives good advice on approaching birds, as well as giving me a ticking-off when I get a bit wayward with my accuracy.

During my shooting life, I have been an extremely bad drawer of positions in the shooting line. However, on this particular day, I drew number 5 in the first drive, which was ideal. The weather was excellent with a light breeze and overcast. At the end of the drive, Jeremy, my loader, remarked that he thought that I had shot well, and said that I had fired 35 shots. I knew that I had killed 28 birds, so I was more than happy with my performance.

The second and third drives were quieter but I still had some good sport and there was plenty of work for Bumble. The last drive before lunch produced a good number of birds and although I was not in the thick of it, I still managed to get 16 partridges. We had just one drive in the afternoon, and as the guns move three places after each drive at Laverstoke, I found myself at number 1. When I discovered where we were going, I was more than happy. My stand was at a cross-section of two hedges at the corner of a field. The birds came in a steady stream, either flying straight over me or going from my left to right. I ended up getting 26, and that was a very big day for me. The bag for the whole day was 201 brace, of which I accounted for 83 birds and fired 135 shots.

GROUSE MOORS ON WHICH I HAVE SHOT

Scotland

Balnacoil
Blair Atholl Castle
Braelangwell
Braemore
Clunes
Conaglen
Dalnamein
Duchally
Dumfries House
Dunrobin
Edradour
Farr
Foich
Glenkyllachy
Glenmazeran
Gordonbush
Invergeldie
Kintradwell
Latheronwheel
Loubcroy
Tongue
Uppat

England

Bolton Abbey
Bolton Castle–Apedale
Bolton Castle–Low Moor
Bolton Castle–West Moor
Caldbergh
Conistone
Coverhead
Crag
East Arkengarthdale
Grassington
Howden Lodge
Marske
Melmerby
Middlesmoor
Mossdale
Scrafton
Thornton Rust

SCOTTISH SALMON RIVERS THAT I HAVE FISHED

Applecross
Arnisdale
Awe
Beauly
Blackwater (Brora)
Blackwater (Carron)
Borgie
Broom
Brora
Carron
Cona
Dee
Deveron
Dionard
Dundonnell
Dyke
Einig
Etive
Findhorn
Garry
Grimersta
Gruinard

Halladale
Iorsa
Kinloch
Kinlochewe
Kyle of Sutherland
Leader Water
Lochy
Machrie
Nairn
Naver
Oykel
South Esk
Spey
Stinchar
Tay
Tilt
Tummel
Tweed
Ullapool

Spey Beats
Arndilly
Ballindalloch
Carron and Laggan
Castle Grant
Gordon Castle
Tulchan
Knockando

Tweed Beats
Birgham Dub
Carham
Lower Floors
Upper Floors
Hendersyde
Lower Makerstoun
Upper Makerstoun
Middle Mertoun
Upper Mertoun
Lower North Wark
Upper Pavilion
Sprouston
South Wark
The Lees

ICELANDIC SALMON RIVERS THAT I HAVE FISHED

Dolum
Grimsa
Haffjardara
Kjarra

Kjos
Langa
Midfjardara

ESTATES THAT I HAVE STALKED ON IN SCOTLAND

Alladale
Applecross
Balnacoil
Ben Alder
Ben More (Mull)
Braelangwell
Braemore
Clunes
Farr

Glen Etive
Glenkyllachy
Glenmazeran
Kinlochewe
Loubcroy
North Drumochter
Skelpick
Tongue

EXTRACTS FROM BOOKS WHICH I HAVE MUCH ENJOYED

THE HIGH TOPS

The High Tops! What magic in the name, what memories they recall. I often wonder if anyone lives who, having once tasted the fascination of their identity, in all a life, however long, forgets it or ceases to think of them as with a certain human fellowship.

I know of no more satisfactory sensation than on a bright morning in September to leave the lower ground as soon after eight as possible, feeling absolutely confident in a glorious prospect of sport and exercise, and to set one's face and best walking powers to the struggle of reaching the 'utmost purple rim' of one of these giant neighbours. No doubt anticipation of the necessary effort, the long, hot pull with the sun beating fiercely on one's head or back, the almost endless ridge after ridge which seem to appear instead of disappear as one slowly crawls upward and onward, is at times rather depressing. Often I have sighed as I looked at the far-off bourne and whispered to myself, 'Shall I ever get there?'. But one does get there, and a great deal farther, before the day is out. Every step ascended seems to be lighter and easier than the last. As the higher ground is gradually reached, the 'going' becomes more and more firm and springy – soon out of the long grass or heather on to the short elastic crop of the Tops, while the spirit rejoices in the sensation of successful energy which leads slowly but surely to the goal of one's efforts.

Once there, can anything be more delicious than the sense of accomplished will? All trifling cares and troubles left far below, life seems altogether on a higher, nobler plateau; and the almost awe-striking realisation of the immensity of nature among the eternal hills fills the mind with solemn rest. Here in these grand surroundings we may consciously feel God walks with man. Let us sit a moment and drink in the charmed aspect. In the far distance to the east are the rolling miles of Rannoch Moor, the hill of Atholl, the peak of mighty Schiehallion's 'Hill of Storms', Corrour, Ben Alder; to the north, Ben Nevis; to the west, Cruachan –

even to the glimmer of the western sea does the prospect lead us. The air up here is fresh and invigorating: in reality it seems a different world from the shadowy valleys lately left below, 'for look how high the heaven is in comparison with the earth'.

Near at hand a brood of gentle ptarmigan are chirping and sunning themselves in the stones. Not yet have they adopted the white garb of winter: they are still clothed in their patterned frocks of brown-and-white. Above us suddenly rises, slowly and majestically, the feathered king of the mountains, the noble eagle, soaring calmly over the sweeping expanse as if it were but a footstep, till he becomes a mere speck on the cloud-line. Even so the little ptarmigan have told each other frightendly of his presence, and have become almost invisible as they crouch among the stones. The hoarse croak of a passing raven makes one look round to see if 'Corrie' has perchance for once forgotten his duties and is barking at some unexpected intrusion, so like a dog's bark is the raven's call. Still we lie on, drinking in by every sense of sight and sound the indescribable beauty, peace, delight, almost ecstasy, of the day and surroundings.

In a quiet meditative way, perhaps one's thoughts turn for the moment to a higher ideal than the beauty of hillside, silver loch, and cloud-flecked heaven, wondering if the everyday of life might not be made more noble, generous, better balanced, if one tried to live it a little nearer the 'Tops' instead of stumbling about so much in the valley of things, as we who live a workaday life mostly do. 'I will lift up mine eyes unto the hills, from whence cometh my help', is certainly a panacea for many of the troubles we magnify and exaggerate, simply because we do not try to rise to a higher level of thought. Often have I heard it remarked, 'What can you find so fascinating in struggling up these hills just at the end to shoot a defenceless stag?' I can hardly explain to questioners such as these that the stag is the least part of it all; that as happy days have been spent on the highest ridges with a good friend and a true telescope, and that the real enjoyment and pleasure consist in the close intercourse with nature – the solitude, the apartness, the constant variation of light and shade, the mystic vagaries of the fleecy clouds, the grandeur of passing storms, the tender sadness of the setting sun leaving his last rosy kiss on the brows of the peaks, and the quiet peace of evening as we turn our steps towards home. Then we feel perhaps we have got just a little bit nearer the truth, because for a brief space we have been treading in truth. These are some of the thoughts that inspire me to write of the 'mountains of my love', so dear for themselves alone, and for many a day of grand sport and adventure, of exercise of wind and limb, of strenuous effort and hardy endurance, which have sent me back to the valleys braced, fortified, and helped to a clearer vision of the immaterial from the material things of life, which were too apt to put in their wrong places – the things that matter from the things which do not matter.

The High Tops of Black Mount, by the Marchioness of Breadalbane

A LADY DEERSTALKER

"Ian," said Sir Aeneas Macpherson, the laird of Dalbeg, as his head stalker stood beside him in the gun-room, "I'm not going out tomorrow. Mrs. Harwood can have my rifle, and you'll take her to Corrie Domhain, if the wind serves."

Ian Mackintosh was one of the old class of stalkers who do not believe in having ladies in the forest, indeed considered them a nuisance, but his master's orders were not to be gainsaid.

"Very well sir. Would you like her to get a good beast?"

"Let her have her chance, Ian. And remember to send her the best head she brings down."

"What, sir, even if she kills the big imperial that's cheated a few of us?"

The laird smiled at the reference to the 14-pointer; moreover Ian had been very unfortunate in his experience with ladies. One had shot a milk-hind, another a knobber, and still another a fawn.

"Oh yes, Ian, I quite understand. But give Mrs. Harwood the same chance as I should have were I out with you. Forget for once her sex. If any stalker can show her sport you're the man."

The other rifles for the morrow having been settled, Ian said good-night, and had a look at the deer larder on his way home. A 9-, a 10- and a 12-pointer, all good beasts, had been the result of the day's stalking. The first had fallen to the laird's own rifle, the others to Major Carpenter, while the Hon. Jack Drummond has cursed his marksmanship in that he had allowed a wounded stag to escape.

The next morning opened well. There was just a suspicion of frost, and a north wind blew, neither too strong nor too weak. Early breakfast at Dalbeg Lodge was the general rule for the rifles, especially when the outlying beasts had to be stalked. The host himself never failed to put in an appearance, whether going out or not. This morning he had three guests at table – Mrs. Harwood, Mr. Drummond and Mr. Frank Derby.

Mrs. Harwood was one of that pleasant class who are as good company at the first meal as at the last. Dressed for the corries in a Lovat mixture, both coat and skirt, as well as boots, were meant for business.

"What about that imperial sir?" asked Derby. "Are we to bring him into the larder today?"

"Certainly, if you can," replied the laird. "Though my neighbour on the east has usually two or three beasts reserved, my stalkers have no such orders."

It was a long and rough road up the glen, so the rifles were off by eight-forty-five, Mrs. Harwood being dropped at the Shepherd's Bridge, where Ian was in waiting with a gillie. Close by was the ponyman with his garron, he doubting much if it should have a back-load that day.

Ian had already spied the position, had had his eye on a mixed parcel over a mile to the westward. So the usual procession was at once formed, he of course leading, the lady at his heels, while the gillie with the rifle and a tracker brought up the rear. An old sheep track was taken advantage of so long as it served. In twenty minutes, however, the heather had to be taken, then a knoll was used as a spying-point to verify the situation of the parcel from which Ian had mentally arranged a toll for his lady. There was no sign of deer, however, so the advance was continued. For fifty yards they had to crawl, and the stalker was not a little astonished at the sporting manner in which the lady got over the ground.

As nothing was yet to be seen, Ian said: "I'm thinking that the beasts have moved away. Just you rest here a bit, madam, and I'll go forward a little by myself and have a good spy."

He seemed gone such a long time that Mrs. Harwood by and by took her own glass, and after a long look she signalled to the gillie to approach.

"What do you see there, Duncan, just to the right of that big white stone, about eighty yards off?"

Duncan, after a careful spy, answered in a whisper: "It's the tips of the horns of a beast asleep, mem. What a chance, if he would only rise. But Ian might not like it."

"Well Duncan, we'll wait a few minutes, and then –"

But nothing happened; the antlers remained motionless.

"Oh, Duncan, how I would like a shot at that stag. Do you think you could get him to stand up?"

"Yes, mem, I could give him my wind. We do not believe in Dalbeg in whistling up stags. But the stalker is away with the cartridges."

"That's all right; just hand me the rifle. I always carry a few in my pocket, so let the beast have your wind."

Duncan set out, casting a wide compass as he came into the wind. Just as Ian appeared from another direction the taint in the wind told, and up got the stag. Ian could see Mrs. Harwood about to fire, so he stood still; evidently the stag had a good head, though he remorsed it was not of his stalking.

The stag stood just long enough for the lady to take steady aim, and the bullet went true. The stalker and the gillie came up together, and lo! there was the much-talked-of imperial. Leaving the gillie to gralloch, Ian hurried to Mrs. Harwood and congratulated her on her marvellous luck. She promptly produced a flask from her Norfolk, so that stalker and gillie might drink the usual toast.

"More blood, madam," said Ian, as he solemnly raised the cup to his lips; "but after your luck before lunch I can scarcely expect to get you a good stag before we go home. I saw nothing when I left you; but we'll wait. Won't the laird be surprised?"

In the stalk after lunch nothing was seen for some time save hinds and a few little beasties, "not worth a shot," as Ian remarked.

"We'll now try Corrie Domhain," said he; "the wind has shifted a bit. But perhaps you've had enough of the hill today?"

"Oh no," was the quick response; "I'd much rather go on. I've heard much of

Corrie Domhain, and also of your great knowledge of deer."

Perseverance seemed certainly about to be rewarded, for there was a small parcel in a position which offered little difficulty. Yet once more Ian was balked, for when he had reduced the distance to two hundred yards two tourists appeared on the scene and the deer bolted.

They were given half-an-hour to settle, then after a slight advance three stags were revealed by the telescope, two of them feeding, the third lying in the heather. As the stalking day was now nearing an end, no delay was made as the party went up a dry watercourse.

A peep was by and by taken of the stags, their position unchanged, but the stalker was in despair. He could get no nearer than one hundred and sixty yards, and what could a lady do at that range?

Getting her alongside, he explained the situation. "I'd like to try a shot," was her answer; "at the worst I can only miss."

"Then take plenty of time," was the injunction; "the one on the left seems the best."

Bang went the rifle – a miss, as Ian had expected. The stags, though thoroughly startled, were yet indecisive what direction to take. "Try again," was his agonised and whispered suggestion, but Mrs. Harwood had already a fresh cartridge in.

Just as the stags had made up their minds she fired, and only two of them went out of sight. Ian was about to tell her to "mak siccar" when the stag, which turned out to be a royal, collapsed.

"Twenty-six points in one day!" exclaimed Ian. "Any sportsman would be proud of such a feat. Surely you have had more experience among deer than I have been thinking."

Thereupon Mrs. Harwood told him her father had so long held Glenmonadh, and that she –

"Oh," interrupted Ian, "you're Miss Beresford that was. I should have remembered. I'm a proud man today; you are the one lady deerstalker I've longed to have a day with on the hill."

Till the moment that the royal fell Ian had been on bad terms with himself and the world; now he went down the hill, Mrs. Harwood taking his arm at the bad bits, the happiest man in Dalbeg forest.

"Well Ian, has the lady disgraced my Mannlicher?" asked the laird, who was waiting when the wagonette arrived.

"Ah sir, you did not tell me that I was having the honour of stalking for Miss Florence Beresford. What a day we've had! Without my help she grassed the imperial that has so often escaped us, and which today I unconsciously walked past; and she finished with a royal at one hundred and sixty yards. It's been her day, though, not mine."

Mrs. Harwood was too good a sportswoman, however, to allow Ian to depart in such a mood.

Deerstalking In Scotland, by A.I. McConnochie